CW01208793

I READ! YOU READ!

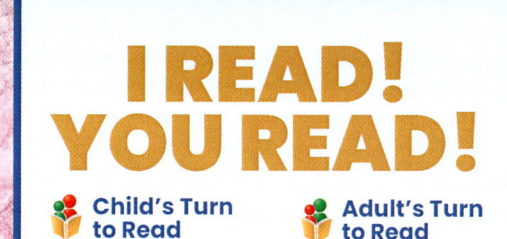

Child's Turn to Read

Adult's Turn to Read

WE READ ABOUT THE Amphibian Life Cycle

Tracy Vonder Brink
and Madison Parker

Table of Contents

Amphibian Life Cycle 3
Words to Know 22
Index 23
Comprehension Questions 23

SEAHORSE PUBLISHING

Parent and Caregiver Guide

Reading aloud with your child has many benefits. It expands vocabulary, sparks discussion, and promotes an emotional bond. Research shows that children who have books read aloud to them have improved language skills, leading to greater school success.

I Read! You Read! books offer a fun and easy way to read with your child. Follow these guidelines.

Before Reading

- Look at the front and back covers. Discuss personal experiences that relate to the topic.
- Read the *Words to Know* at the back of the book. Talk about what the words mean.
- If the book will be challenging or unfamiliar to your child, read it aloud by yourself the first time. Then, invite your child to participate in a second reading.

During Reading

CHILD Have your child read the words beside this symbol. This text has been carefully matched to the reading and grade levels shown on the cover.

ADULT You read the words beside this symbol.

- Stop often to discuss what you are reading and to make sure your child understands.
- If your child struggles with decoding a word, help them sound it out. If it is still a challenge, say the word for your child and have them repeat it after you.
- To find the meaning of a word, look for clues in the surrounding words and pictures.

After Reading

- Praise your child's efforts. Notice how they have grown as a reader.
- Use the *Comprehension Questions* at the back of the book.
- Discuss what your child learned and what they liked or didn't like about the book.

Most importantly, let your child know that reading is fun and worthwhile. Keep reading together as your child's skills and confidence grow.

Amphibian Life Cycle

All living things are born.

They grow to be adults.

We call these changes a life cycle.

A life cycle is all the steps in the life of a living thing. As an animal or a plant grows up, it goes through changes in each step of its life cycle.

Amphibians are animals with backbones.

They live part of their lives in water and part on land.

Amphibians are **cold-blooded**.

Since amphibians have a backbone, they are vertebrates. Reptiles, birds, and mammals are also vertebrates.

Amphibians also have smooth skin.

An amphibian's life cycle begins with an egg.

An **embryo** grows inside.

Frog eggs absorb the water around them and become a jelly. The jelly protects them from predators and keeps them from floating away.

Most amphibians lay their eggs in water.

The embryo becomes a **larva**.

The larva hatches from the egg.

A tadpole is the larva of a frog or a toad.

It takes about 14 weeks for tadpoles to become little frogs or toads. Tadpoles must stay in the water and eat a lot of food like algae.

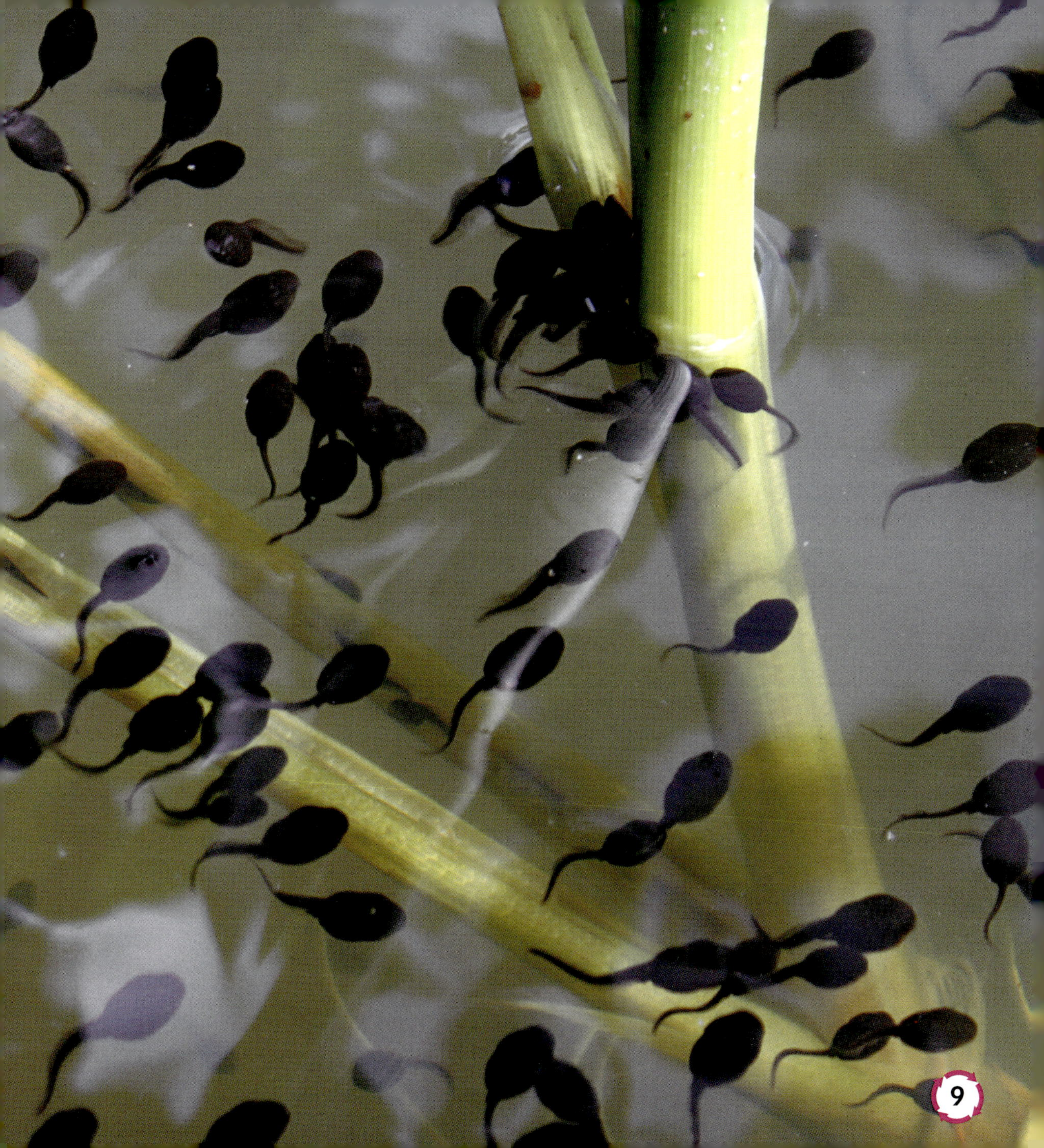

10

A tadpole lives in water.

It has a tail.

It breathes underwater through **gills**.

Gills are organs in a water animal's body. Gills take oxygen from the water so the animal can breathe.

A tadpole grows legs.

It grows **lungs** to breathe air.

We call these big changes a **metamorphosis**.

When an animal goes through **metamorphosis**, there is a major change in the animal's body structure as it becomes an adult.

ADULT

Salamanders do not lose their tails during metamorphosis.

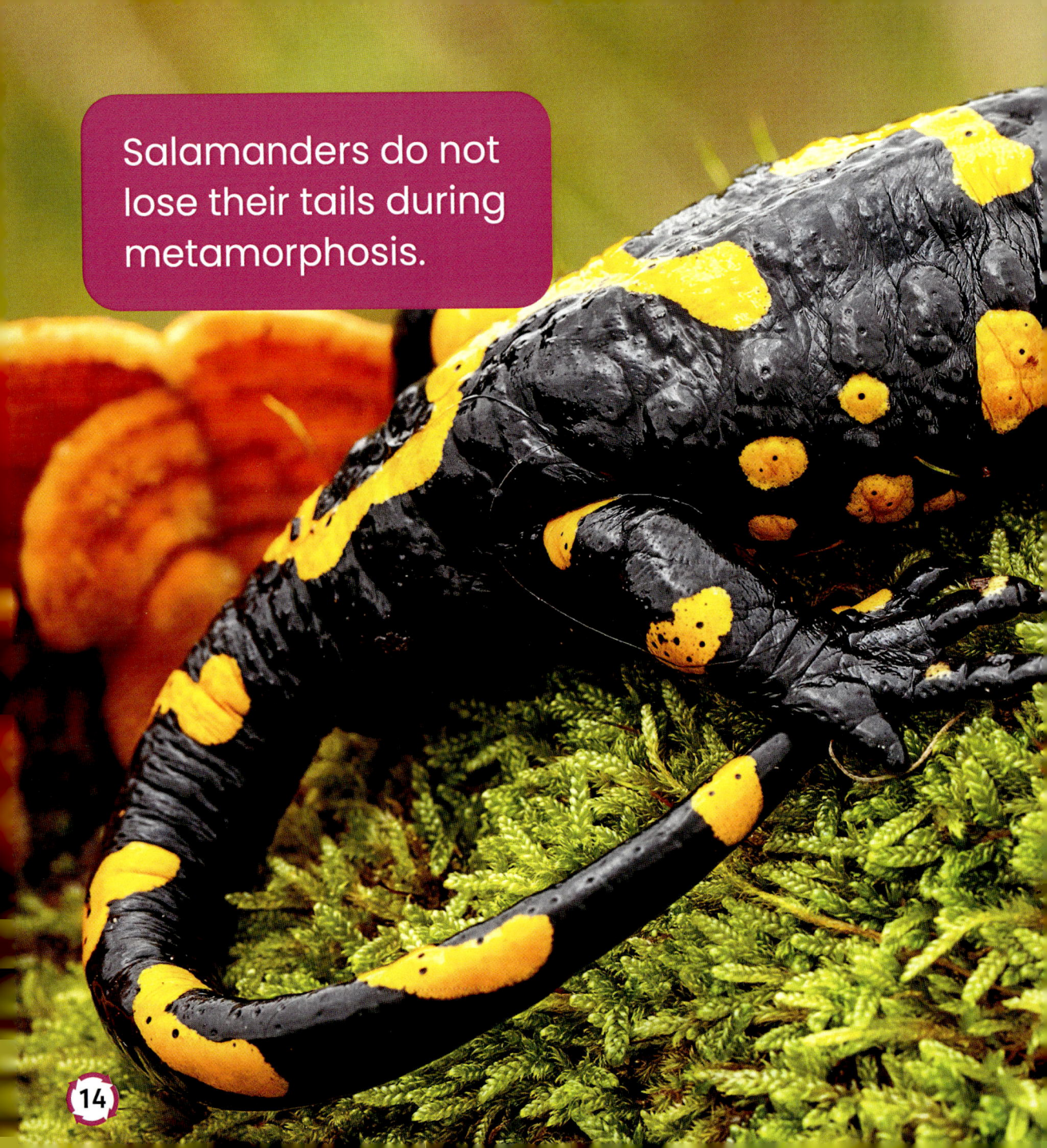

Salamanders are amphibians like frogs and toads.

Salamanders also go through metamorphosis.

A salamander **larva** hatches from an egg. Just like a tadpole, it has a tail. It must stay in the water until its body changes.

Amphibians can leave the water after they grow legs and lungs.

They are able to live on land.

CHILD

Frogs can live on land and in water. They are semiaquatic. Some salamanders are also semiaquatic.

ADULT

17

The skin on a frog's throat puffs out to make his call louder.

Adult amphibians find mates.

Some males call to females.

The females look for the loudest male.

Since mating takes place at night, the female sings a duet with the male to help find him in the dark.

The females lay eggs.

The life cycle begins again.

A life cycle is sometimes called the circle of life. The pattern repeats over and over again.

ADULT

Words to Know

cold-blooded (kohld BLUHD-id): unable to make body heat; having a body temperature that changes with the temperature of the surroundings

embryo (EM-bree-oh): a living creature in the earliest stage of development, before it is hatched or born

gills (gilz): body parts near the mouth in fish and other living creatures that allow them to breathe underwater

larva (LAHR-vuh): a stage in the development of many living creatures that happens between birth or hatching and before adulthood

lungs (luhngz): body parts that people and some animals use to breathe air

metamorphosis (met-uh-MOR-fuh-sis): a major change in the form and appearance of some living creatures that happens as they become adults

Index

egg(s) 6, 7, 8, 15, 20
frog(s/'s) 6, 8, 15, 16, 18
larva 8, 15

metamorphosis 12–15
salamanders 14–16
tadpole 8, 11, 12, 15

Comprehension Questions

1. An amphibian's life cycle begins with
   a. a larva.   b. an egg.   c. a metamorphosis.
2. A tadpole is the larva of
   a. a salamander.
   b. a crocodile.
   c. a frog or a toad.
3. Amphibians can leave the water after they grow
   a. a tail and gills.
   b. an embryo and an egg.
   c. legs and lungs.
4. **True or false:** Amphibians are not able to live on land.
5. **True or false:** Amphibians go through metamorphosis when they grow legs and lungs.

Answers: 1.b 2.c 3.c 4.False 5.True

Written by: Tracy Vonder Brink and Madison Parker
Design by: Bobbie Houser
Editor: Kim Thompson

Library of Congress PCN Data
We Read About the Amphibian Life Cycle / Tracy Vonder Brink and Madison Parker
I Read! You Read!
ISBN 979-8-8873-5192-6 (hard cover)
ISBN 979-8-8873-5212-1 (paperback)
ISBN 979-8-8873-5232-9 (EPUB)
ISBN 979-8-8873-5252-7 (eBook)
Library of Congress Control Number: 2022945531

Printed in the United States of America.

Photographs:
t = Top, b = Bottom, c = Center, l = Left, r = Right

Shutterstock: Tod Walker: cover tl; Suwat wongkham: cover tr; MLHoward: cover b; Creeping Things: p. 3; Rudmer Zwerver: p. 5 t; WildMedia: pp. 5 b, 14-15; Artur Bociarski: pp. 6-7; Robirensi: pp. 8-9; Deborah Lee Rossiter: p. 10; W. de Vries: pp. 12-13; Kurit afshen: p. 17; Awei: p. 18; Doksya: pp. 20-21

Seahorse Publishing Company

www.seahorsepub.com

Copyright © 2023 **SEAHORSE PUBLISHING COMPANY**

All rights reserved. No part of this publication may be reproduced, stored in a retrieval system or be transmitted in any form or by any means, electronic, mechanical, photocopying, recording, or otherwise, without the prior written permission of Seahorse Publishing Company.

Published in the United States
Seahorse Publishing
PO Box 771325
Coral Springs, FL 33077